Sardinia
Travel Guide

Quick Trips Series

Table of Contents

Sardinia

Located in the Mediterranean Sea, the island of Sardinia is filled with pleasant contrasts. The glitzy Costa Smeralda is dotted with boutique hotels and posh beaches and is full of five-star glamour. Meanwhile Sardinia has a charming interior with tiny untouched villages. Stretches of enclosed swimming areas along the coast and unexplored coves are just waiting to be discovered.

Off the coast, Sardinia is filled with eccentric ruins and archeological remnants all attesting to the island's "Nuragic" heritage. (Nuraghe are megalithic columns from the Bronze Era.)

The large valleys, rising peaks, and winding trails make for great day trip excursions. And don't miss the amazing diversity of seafood, cozy cafes and street-front restaurants. If you are looking to get away from mainland Italy the beauty of Sardinia will not disappoint you.

🌍 Geography

Sardinia is the second biggest island in the Mediterranean, after Sicily. It is an independent area of Italy with the closest islands being Corsica, Sicily and the Spanish Balearic Islands. The area of Sardinia, whose capital is Cagliari, covers 23, 821 km square while the coastline runs for an estimated 1,849 km.

A rocky and hilly geology, several large bays, inlets, rias and smaller islands along the coast characterize the coast of Sardinia. The highest point in the island is Punta La

Marmora at 1834 metres; it is a component of the Gennargentu Mountains. Other nearby mountain peaks are Monte Limbara, Monte Alba, Monte Linas, the Sette Fratelli, the Chain of Marghine as well as the Sulcis mountains.

The island of Sardinia is the fourth least populated area in Italy. The population density stands at about 69 km square (and has significantly low fertility and birth rates.) These demographic trends combined with the high urbanization in the island have allowed for the preservation of large natural reservations.

Sardinia's people have historically been wary of foreign developments especially along the coast – and the island has a history of frequent raids! Nevertheless, due to the increasing popularity of the island's coast, seaside tourism is at its peak and many urban centers can be found along the coast, leaving the inland sparingly populated.

The major populations on the island are from Eastern Europe, China and Africa. Others are from nearby Corsica, Spain, and parts of North Africa. In 2010, the island hosted more than 36,000 foreign residents, accounting for up to 2.3% of the island's total population.

🌎 Customs & Culture

The island of Sardinia boasts a vibrant and ancient history. The Nuraghi Romanian ruins and fortresses that date as far back as 3500 years attest to this rich history. These ruins are scattered all over the island and serve as a reminder of Sardinia's prehistoric inhabitants and their culture. The city of Alghero highlights both Romanian and

Catalan history with its cobbled walkways, lighthouses, enclosed towns and architectural attractions.

🌍 Language

The official language in the island is Italiano (Italian). However, Sardinian or Sardu is widely spoken among the locals.

The language is largely derived from Romanian influences and borrows from Catalan, native Nuragic, Phoenician and Spanish. Campidanese (Sardu Campidanesu) and Logudorese (Sardu Logudoresu) are the most widely spoken Sardinian dialects in the island. Campidanese is limited to the southern parts of Sardinia while Logudorese in popular in the northern and central areas of the island.

This diversity in language has led to the gradual creation of various language communities. For example in the capital city, people speak a different strain of Catalan, commonly known as Alguerés or Algherese. In the smaller island of Sant'Antioco and San Pietro, Tabarchino (Tabarchin) is widely spoken.

Other smaller groups in the island speak Fertilia, Friulian and Venetian and other local dialects. To the visitor, the difference in dialects may not be evident but as you stay longer on the island, you just might start noticing the differences!

🌍 Music & Festivals

Music has a special place in Sardinian life. Often processions line up the streets with the locals dancing, playing instruments and creating harmonious music. Both the old and the young are involved in preserving their musical heritage.

The island boasts well-known jazz musicians such as Paolo Fresu and Marcello Melis. Other popular musicians are Elena Ledda and Maria Carta. The major opera theaters are Teatro Auditorium Comunale and the Teatro Lirico in Sassari and Cagliari respectively.

Many of the festivals in Sardinia are religious while others are dedicated to the harvest. The artichoke festival held in Uri in March and the cherry festival held in Nuoro in June are some of the most popular festivals on the island. Other spectacular fetes include the L'Ardia Horse Race held in Sedilo every July and the Sa Sartiglia Carnival hosted in Oristano in February.

 Cuisine

In the spirit of Italy and neighbouring Mediterranean islands, food is celebrated in Sardinia. Seafood, sardines, tuna, strong cheese and bottarga are some of the most loved foods in the island. Others include roasted pork, wild game (boiled or stir-fried with beans), vegetables and homemade leavened breads such as coccoi piñatas and pistoccu. Freshly ground herbs and spices are used to add zest to the food, with the most favored being basil, garlic, and oregano.

Weather & Best Time to Visit

The island of Sardinia has wonderful summers that last for 6 months from May to October. The early months of summer are particularly pleasant due to the incoming breeze from the Mediterranean. The best time to go is between May and June when the skies are clear and the sun is not sweltering. The weather at this time averages

between 220C (71F) and 250C (77F).

August is the hottest time to visit, given the scorching sun

and is busy with crowds that flood the coast. The winters

are generally mild with intervals of sunshine, especially in

the months of March and April. However, the slight rain

and snow in winter may see many resorts and tourist

areas closed until Easter.

Sights & Activities: What to See & Do

🌐 Grotta Di Nettuno Marine Cave

Grotta di Nettuno (Neptune's Grotto) are marine caves situated to the west of Alghero town. The caves are popular tourist attractions due to their ease of accessibility and the magnificent views these caves offer. They are reachable by road and by boat.

SARDINIA TRAVEL GUIDE

Grotta di Nettuno was discovered by eighteenth century fishermen. Today, the cave is lit to highlight the dramatic formations within the hollows of the cave. The structures take the form of cathedral pillars and musical instruments and the caves are named after these shapes.

It is best to arrive early at the caves' entrance to ensure that you do not miss the tour that takes place each hour. This guided tour of the caves lasts 45 minutes and entails an exploration of the cave system and an explanation of its formation by a tour guide.

The boat departs from Alghero to the Grotto on an hourly basis. These trips cost $12 in addition to the $12 charged at the entrance on arrival at Grotto. The boat trip takes about two hours and thirty minutes. The attractive sea voyage is worth the cost. Visitors will enjoy the luminous

SARDINIA TRAVEL GUIDE

Port Conte bay and the breathtaking rocks of Capo Caccia.

The road to the Grotto usually gets crowded in the summer months. However, visitors can park on roadside where the trail ends and take a short walk to the caves. There are up to 65 stairways that lead to the cave system; these are equally rewarding and they offer a worthwhile "exercise" to visitors.

These zigzag steps are also known as the goat's steps (Escala del Cabirol). They were formed within the cliff in the early 1950s and it takes up to 15 minutes to ascend. On windy days, the sight of the sea smashing into the cliff wall is a sight to see.

Address: Capo Caccia, Alghero, Sardinia

🌍 Cittadella Dei Musei (Citadel of Museums)

The Citadel of Museums is located in the town of Cagliari to the northwest of the dell'Indipendenza Piazza. Sitting on a limestone hills, it is one of the best-known museums on the island and hosts the sixteenth century displays of the Palearo brothers and Rocco Cappellino.

Between the sixteenth and the eighteenth centuries, the Citadel of Museums served as a storage arsenal, as a prison and later as a military barracks. It was heavily damaged during the Second World War and was restored in the 1960s to host its various museums and exhibitions. Some major museums hosted within the citadel are the National Gallery (Pinacoteca Nazionale), the National Archeological Museum, the Museum of Siamese Art and the Wax Anatomical Models Museum.

The city of Cagliari is a delight in itself. It is home to remodeled ancient churches, pastel buildings, parks and lush botanic gardens that serve as nearby attractions. Just close to the museums are various cafes and restaurants that offer a great view of the city of Cagliari.

Address: Viale Regian Elena, 09124, Cagliari

Open: 9am daily except Sunday

Phone: +39 070 6757000

 Bosa Town

Bosa is an ancient marine town located just forty kilometers south of the city of Alghero. Until recently, this town was the only one the Nuoro coast. In 2005, following a reshuffling of the provinces in Sardinia, Bosa was incorporated into the province of Oristano. From Alghero, Bosa can be accessed by road or by boat.

The town is situated 5km on the mainland from River Temo, the only navigable river on the island. The town is enclosed within mountain ranges and the sea and has very few touristic developments. As such, Bosa offers a tranquil, unhurried atmosphere.

The ancient citadel of Castello Malaspina is visible from virtually every angle in Bosa. The influential Malaspina ancestors built this citadel in 1112. The only remains are the enclosing wall and the Nostra Signora di Regnos Altos church.

The Bosa marina attracts many visitors looking to enjoy the sights of the sea while relaxing in the quiet beaches.

Cozy cafes, restaurants and Italian style bars, also line the marina. It is also an excellent spot for water activities and sun bathing.

Address: Oristano 08013, Sardinia, Italy

🌍 Golfo Di Orosei (Gulf Of Orosei)

The Golfo di Orosei (Gulf of Orosei) is located in the province of Ogliastra. This stretch of wild beaches and coves attracts nature lovers looking to get away from the crowded beaches. The coast can be reached easily from the mainland through boat excursions.

The boat trip offers impressive sights of the ancient caves, unexplored coves and rugged cliffs that hang over the sea. Some of the most attractive coastlines are in

Cala Gonone and in Santa Maria Navarrese. Here, the coast is free of inhabitants and only a majestic hinterland covered by wild flora and fauna takes over the gulf.

The Foca Monaca or the nun seal is an extinct mammal that attracts many visitors to this part of the sea. Another attraction is the Cala Luna, a wide sandy beach hidden among oleanders and the overhanging cliffs around the sea. The Goloritzé is a formidable limestone peak that watches over the golden beach of Capo di Monte Santo.

Several meters from the beach, is a stone structure that protrudes from the water to form an arc. Hunting, hiking and camping excursions along the beach and inland are prohibited. This ensures that the delicate ecosystem along the Gulf is maintained.

Address: Orosei, Nuoro, Sardinia

🌍 Tharros Archeological Site

Tharros is a medieval port located in the province of Oristano in Sardinia. The port, with its Phoenician and Roman heritage protrudes into the sea to create a natural reef for the Oristano bay. The port is surrounded by white beaches with the Arutas claimed to be the cleanest beach in Italy.

In addition to the attractive beaches, Tharros offers an open archeological strip. There are no guided tours to take visitors through the archeological sites. However, several ruins offer a great daytime escape from the bustling beaches. From the ruins, a dive into the sea is just close by.

The nearby Archaeological Museum in Cagliari offers an organized display of the excavations from Tharros. Cabras, only 9 km from Tharros hosts another museum which hosts the ancient cultural artifacts of Tharros.

Another nearby attraction is San Salvatore, a tiny town that is a favorite of Western-Italian films. The Festival of San Salvatore also known as Santu Sabradore is just as rewarding. The festival takes place on the first Saturday of September and features young lads covered in robes running bare foot while carrying the San Salvatore statute. The celebration is a commemoration of the preservation of the statute that was saved from destruction during the Saracen battles.

Address: San Giovanni di Sinis, Cabras Province of

Oristano

🌍 Gorropu Gorge

The Gorropu Gorge is the deepest gorge in Europe. The

Flumineddu stream cuts through the Supra Monte and

divides it into two to form the Gorge. Impressively, the

Flumineddu flows for 1km through the rocky walls that rise

400m from the stream's base.

The unceasing flow of the river has also created an

underground cave beneath rocky walls. Exploring the

Gorrupo Gorge past the cave will require special gear for

maneuvering the canyon. From the valley, visitors can

hike up most of the gorge through the large cobblestones.

The ascending trip offers breathtaking views of the valley

below as well as the surrounding cliffs.

As one descends the gorge on the other side, there are small glittering lakes enclosed within weathered rocks. From here, you can see the meeting of the Flumineddu and the Codula Orbisi cave. The cave can only be accessed from one side of the gorge.

Address: Dorgali, Nuoro

Arzachena

The resort town of Arzachena is located south of La Maddalena island on the northeast side of Sardinia. Arzachena features up to 80 kilometers of wild beaches characterized by jutting rocks and tranquil coves that can be reached by boat.

Other than the attractive beaches, the archeological attractions of Arzachena are some of the most compelling in Sardinia. One such attraction is the nuraghe that are scattered all over Sardinia.

The graves or Tombs Of Giants are impressive sites that evoke the memories of the legendry inhabitants of this region. The massive tombs, which was once a communal burial area comprises of a channel that is covered by wood and bronze that was used to lower the dead to the burial grounds.

Address: Olbia-Tempio 07021, Sardinia

🌐 Garibaldi's House & Museum

Garibaldi's House is a popular stop when visitors explore the small island of Caprera in Sardinia. Garibaldi's House and Museum host the memories of the revolutionary and national hero Giuseppe Garibaldi. After a failed attempt to take over Sicily and Naples, he fled to mainland Italy in the 1800s. He spent his final years in the island of Caprera and died in 1882.

The house has been left in the same state since his demise. The statute of Garibaldi stands in front of this house while olive plantations flank his tomb at the back of the house. On the anniversary of Giuseppe Garibaldi's death the house and museum is often visited by many local and international visitors.

Address: Caprera Island, Sardinia

Open: Daily

🌐 Sant' Antioco & San Pietro Islands

Sant' Antioco and San Pietro Islands are some of the most magnificent in Sardinia. Sant'Antioco is the fourth largest island in Italy and covers an estimated 109 square kilometers. Santa Caterina links the island to the mainland of Sardinia.

Santa Caterina is a man-made protrusion of land that extends 3 km into the sea. It is believed that the Carthaginians first created this bridge and the Romans later developed it further. As you pass through the boardwalk from the mainland of Sardinia, you can still see ancient Roman arches.

Today, Sant'Antioco offers a rich archeological heritage. Medieval shrines, tablets from the Hebrews and a necropolis can be seen. The catacombs at the base of the old church at St. Antioco are of particular interest. The necropolis was a burial site for stillborn children and the grounds where younger children were offered as sacrifices.

Another attraction worth a visit is the Antiquarium. This museum hosts Roman and Phoenician medieval poetry, jewelry and urns from the nearby necropolis. The Castello Sabaudo overlooks the town of Sant'Antioco. This red walled small town was built in the sixteenth century. The reconstructed town features promenades shaded by trees, bars, shops and cafes that come to life in the evenings.

The small port nearby provides boat excursions around the island and to the neighboring San Pietro. San Pietro derived its name from Jesus' disciple, Peter. It is said that the apostle Peter stayed at the shore of the island briefly on his way to Rome. The town was largely uninhabited until 1738 when local fishermen from Pegli took over the island.

Nearby attractions, include Le Colonne, a large edifice lying on the southern end of the island. The southeastern side of the island is studded by alluring beaches, sand dunes and lagoons hosting exotic bird species such as the Corsican gulls and kestrels.

Carloforte hosts up to 6600 inhabitants and boasts colored houses that evoke the memories of earlier Ligurian times. It also features tree-lined promenades and avenues that overlook the marina. The old tuna fishery offers informative displays of the island's tuna industry and history. Carloforte can be reached by ferry in about forty-five minutes from Calasetta or from the Sardinian mainland at Portovesme.

Address: Province of Carbonia-Iglesias 09017, Sardinia, Italy

🌍 Nora Town

Nora Town is located to the southwest of Cagliari. The history of this ancient and picturesque town dates as far back as the eighth century AD. It is claimed to be the first town on the island and its first inhabitants were the Nuraghic people, who began settling at the nearby Pula peninsula.

The Phoenicians colonized the town of Nora, not violently but instead as traders. The town was an ideal port that would provide adequate shelter during bad weather.

Later, Nora fell under Roman rule after the Romans took

control of Sardinia in 238 BC. The early colonizers then abandoned the town in the eighth century.

The southern tip of the island of Sardinia continues to sink into the Sea. As such, most of the former Nora town has sunk into the sea as well. This has also happened to the former ancient city of Bithia that is close by Nora. The whole of Bithia is under water.

The remaining parts of Nora make for an interesting archeological attraction. The remains of its Roman, Carthaginian and Phoenician settlers are the major highlights in this town. The archeological zone displays prehistoric ruins, tiny homes and villas, thermal pools and the old Romanian theater that hosts several summer performances.

Other nearby attraction is Pula, a small town with an impressive array of streets lined with shops and pastel colored houses. Capo Spartivento beach is a major attraction for water sports lovers and sun worshipers. It also boasts some of the island's largest sand dunes.

Visiting Nora's archeological zone serves as a worthwhile side trip when you Cagliari.

Address: Nora Archaeological Site, nr. Pula, Sardinia

Open: 9am daily throughout the year

Phone: 070 921470

🌏 Giara Di Gesturi Plateau

The Giara di Gesturi is located next to the town of Gesturi at the heart of the Sardinian mainland. These are plateaus made from weathered basalt and rise suddenly from the island's plains. They are exhibited as huge fortresses stretching for over 45 kilometers square and rise to 600m high.

After going past the world heritage site at Burumini, go straight into Gesturi and follow the plaques pointing to Giara. The plateau has a distinctively different ecosystem from the rest of the island. The area exhibits a combination of exotic flora and fauna, wild horses, and pools of lakes scattered across the plain.

Interesting attractions are the wild horses believed to be the only such species in Europe. The increasingly threatened wild horses that roam the Giara are small and covered with dark hair. They live in groups of seven or eight and number to about 500.

The Giara is also known for its cork trees and a lot of cork harvesting takes place here. Sardinian is the highest producer of cork globally. It is an incredible site to see large amounts of cork harvested and piled up in high stacks.

It is possible to hike up the Giara but it is just as rewarding to take a horse ride to explore the wonders of this expansive fortress. A knowledgeable tour guide leads the excursion in Giara and although he speaks only in Sardinian and Italian, the excursion is worthwhile.

🌎 Monte Ortobene Mountain

Monte Ortobene is located just 7km northeast of Nuoro town. A gigantic statue of Christ the Redeemer (Redentore) flanks the granite mountain that rises to

955m. The mountain area is popular with picnicers and the spiritually focused.

This famous statue was set up in 1901 following Pope Leo XIII's decree to raise 19 statues across Italy to mark 19 centuries of the Christian religion in the country. The statue shows the Christ crushing the devil beneath his feet and it has become a spot for pilgrims seeking cures and a solution to their day-to-day challenges.

On August 29 each year, worshipers draped in colorful robes hold a pilgrimage here very early in the morning. This is followed by a mass celebration at the nearby Chiesa di Nostra Signora del Monte and another mass is held late the next morning at the foot of the Redentore.

SARDINIA TRAVEL GUIDE

Visitors looking for a quiet, lush area to have a picnic or for a different experience away from the beaches, Monte Ortobene is an ideal spot. There are several restaurants and bars around the area offering light snacks, meals and drinks.

The road that leads to this pious peak is as rewarding as the peak itself. From the road you can see spectacular views of the large valley in Oliena and Mount Corrasi. There are buses that transport visitors to the mountain area from the Vittorio Emanuele Piazza from morning to about 8.30pm.

Address: Nuoro, Sardinia

◐ Tiscali Village

Tiscali is an old, mysterious village located in the valley of Lanaittu between Dorgali and Oliena. The village was built within the enclosures of the Supramonte, which hosts several caves that were formed through weather processes.

The Supramonte mountain ranges that houses the village is made of limestone stones that date as far back as 180 million years ago. The cave villages were formed through the Karst phenomenon that took place over millions of years.

The early presence of humans in the area can be traced back to the remains in the Lanaittu valley at the bottom of the Supramonte. The excavated remains show that the early inhabitants of these mountain dwellings lived here almost 1400 years ago. It is believed that the early

inhabitants of the Lanaittu valley moved into the mountain

and built the Tiscali village because of raids during the

Roman invasion.

The mountain village of Tiscali is characterized by two

sets of huts. The first set is made up of roughly 40 huts

and is located close to the mountain entrance. The

second set of huts lies to the southwest part of the caves.

They are smaller yet whole families inhabited them; they

seem more like granaries than domestic units.

Address: Nuoro Town, Dorgali Village

🌐 Su Nuraxi di Barumini (UNESCO World Heritage Site)

The Su Nuraxi di Barumini or the Barumini Nuraghe is situated in Barumini, approximately 65 kilometers to the north of Cagliari. It is a UNESCO world heritage site and a popular demonstration of the nuraghe that dot the island of Sardinia. The nuragic complex in Barumini comprises the nuraghe as well as the small town.

Nuraghi, are megalithic columns of the Bronze Era. These towers are found within villages. The utility of these massive columns is not certain, as there is very little historical literature about the nuragic people. There are up to 7000 such towers in the island but many of them are now ruined.

Barumini is accessible by car and there are no public buses directly to Su Nuraxi. However, the public buses will take you to Barumini town and visitors can then walk one mile to reach the Su Nuraxi nuraghe. Guided tours are available and take place every thirty minutes. It is best to book a guide in advance.

Address: From Cagliari, take the SS 131 to the SS 197 route.

Open: 9am daily throughout the year

Cost: $12 for a ticket to visit the Zapata nuraghe and the museum in Barumini town.

Budget Tips

🌐 Accommodation

Luna E Limoni

Luna E Limoni is a charming bed and breakfast suitable

for those looking for elegance at a pocket friendly price.

The hotel is located in the small village of Muravera to the

south east of the island. It is closely situated to natural

attractions such as the Capo Ferrator, several nuraghe and the Costa Rei beach.

The rooms are cozy, clean and offer a free internet connection. The outdoor garden is serene and ideal for an evening glass of wine. The host and owner, Marina, is very knowledgeable about the village and offers great insights for daytime excursions. This small bed and breakfast is close to several street cafes, restaurants and bars.

Address: Via Roma 134 Vico Giardini 4, 09043 Muravera, Sardinia, Italy

Phone: 070 9930703/0039 347 5256646

Price: Starting from $54 per person per night

Website: http://www.lunaelimoni.it/

Sas Abbilas Agriturismo

Sas Abbilas Agriturismo is roughly 10km from Bonorva and offers a different experience for the visitor to Sardinia. The small hotel is located deep in the farms of Bonorva and offers locally made and fresh food in addition to pleasant accommodation.

The nearby countryside offers a different experience to the beaches. Visitors can relax in the lush fields and then return to the hotel where freshly prepared food and wine awaits you. The menu includes pastas, local sausages, pancetta, and cheeses, just to mention a few.

There are only a few rooms available and it is best to check whether there are any left before visiting. Most nights it will just be a few guests and the talkative but friendly farm owners at the Sas Abbilas Agriturismo.

Address: Mariani, 07012 Bonorva, Sardinia

Phone: +39 347 6758725

Price: starting $36

Brezza Marina

Brezza Marina is a self-catering rental apartment block located in Torre dei Corsari. The rooms have recently been refurbished to accommodate double beds in addition to the single bed villas. Although the rooms do not have air conditioning, they are thoughtfully decorated and are kept clean.

The hotel is close to the lively beach, which is just 300 metres away. It also has close proximity to several pizza cafes, supermarkets and restaurants. It is an ideal place for the traveler looking for a private getaway that allows for beach excursions, reliable self-catering and access to the local restaurants.

Address: Torre dei Corsari snc 09031 Arbus

Phone: 39.338.3676886

Website: http://www.brezzamarina.it/

Price: Starting $50

Le Tre Querce

Le Tre Querce is a picturesque resort located in San Teodoro. The rooms are well kept and are furnished with modern amenities including comfortable beds, clean linen bed covers and fresh towels. The rooms are also fitted with clean shower rooms and a kitchenette, ideal for the self-catering traveler. Rooms open up to a well-kept terrace.

The pool is a main attraction; it is large, not crowded and clean. If you are not looking to go to the bustling beaches, the pool will be adequate.

Address: Via La Canna, snc 8020

San Teodoro, Sardinia

Phone: +39 0784869082

Website: www.letrequerce.it/inglese/

Price: starting $678 per week for two people

Corallo Hotel

The Corallo hotel is just 1km from the archeological seaside center of Posada. The Corallo is a small, clean family-run hotel that offers a pleasant getaway at pocket-friendly prices. Visitors looking to escape the bustling beach resorts and city will appreciate this hotel. The hotel is near to the beach, town attractions and the airport.

The rooms are big enough to accommodate two people. It also has single rooms for the independent traveler. Each room is furnished with basic furniture, air-conditioning and sparkling bathrooms. The restaurant is equally small and cozy, accommodating only a few people at a time. The meals offered are light with vegetarian and non-vegetarian options.

Address: Posada – Nuoro, Via Londra, 1, Sardinia

Phone: 0784 812030 / 348 0807504

Website: www.hotel-corallo-sardegna.eu/italiano

Price: Double room, B&B $71 or half board $119. Prices

are per room

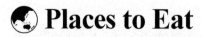 Places to Eat

Antica Trattoria (Olbia)

Antica Trattoria is for the romantically inclined. It is tiny,

sweet place that has tried to maintain its local features

and without being too touristic. The menus have a fixed

price that is affordable for the independent traveler. The

daily buffet is especially appetizing and offers some of the

best pastas and pizza slices. The charming front garden

allows for al fresco dining.

Address: Via delle Terme 1, Olbia centre

Contact: 00 39 0789 24053

Open: Tue–Sun, 12.30pm–2.45pm; 7.30pm–11.30pm.

Ristorante Friggitoria La Saletta (Alghero)

If you want to experience traditional Sardinian cuisine then Ristorante Friggitoria La Saletta is the perfect dining place. Although the menu is somewhat limited, the food is prepared to perfection. The menu features both Italian and English cuisines with many local Sardinian specialties.

The owner is very warm and makes the whole experience all the more enjoyable. It is a good idea to book in advance to avoid disappointment. The homemade food, priced reasonably makes Ristorante Friggitoria La Saletta very popular among travelers and the islanders.

Address: Via Kennedy 27B, 07041 Alghero, Sardinia

Phone: 3492223337

Trattoria Maristella (Alghero)

Trattoria Maristella is a warm restaurant at the heart of Alghero owned by a local patron and offering traditional foods. It is hidden between the tower at Sullis and the movie theatre. The restaurant is very popular with the locals and gets busy in the evenings and at lunchtime.

The wide variety of meats including lamb and pork and the wine selection is reasonably priced.

Address: Via Kennedy, 9, Alghero, 07041

Phone: +39 079978172

Open: Daily

Su Cumbidu (Cagliari)

The Su Cumbidu located in Cagliari is the perfect spot for the traveler looking for a laidback atmosphere without the swish of highly priced restaurants that are typical of the capital. This restaurant resembles a massive rustic wine vault and the atmosphere inside is alluring.

Pass by here for a quick lunch or a more leisurely Sardinian dinner. The meals are fixed-price with up to five local menus to choose from. Su Cumbidu tends to get crowded at lunchtime and in the evening, attracting a younger Italian crowd.

Address: Via Napoli 11

Phone: 00 39 070 660017

Open: Daily, 1pm–3pm and 7pm–11pm

Bella E Monella (Arzachena)

Bella E Monella is a small but cozy restaurant in Arzachena town. It is ideal for lunch or a romantic dinner for those looking for authentic homemade cuisines. They offer a wide array of freshly made breads, salads and the highlight is their spicy inferno pizza. The deserts are top notch, especially the tiramisu that is best for the hot summer season.

The seafood is not delicately presented but it has the authentic taste of Sardinia. The lobsters and oysters are brought directly from the sea and prepared to order. The service here is especially friendly.

Address: Cascioni 3km Strada Provincale per Porto Cervo, 07021 Arzachena, Sardinia

Phone: 0039 3473327896

Open: Daily

 Shopping

Cagliari

The capital of Sardinia has plenty of great places to shop for the budget traveler. Away from the boutique shops along Largo Carlo Felice and Via Roma, visitors looking for a more traditional fare can stroll the streets of Manno and Vias Garibaldi.

The stalls along these streets sell traditional artwork, colorful jewelry and accessories as well as reasonably priced clothes. The small but vibrant open-air market in Santa Clara is a popular visit. It is the oldest market in Cagliari and it is situated in the historical square behind Piazza Yenne.

Market Address: Scalette Santa Chiara, Piazza Yenne

Open: Monday to Saturday 7am to 2pm

San Benedetto Market

The San Benedetto Market in Cagliari is an impressive shopping spot. Built in the 1950s, the market has two stories and covers an area of approximately 4000 square meters. Each of the two floors feature stalls offering an attractive display of products. It is one of the largest markets in Europe.

On the lower floor, there is a wide array of seafood including lobster, octopus, oyster and crab. The other floor is dedicated to clothing, jewelry, shoes, and artworks.

Address: Via Francesco Cocco Ortu, 50 (Via Tiziano), Cagliari, Sardegna 09128

Open: Monday to Saturday 8am to 2pm

Oristano

Visitors looking to explore Sardinian markets will not be disappointed by the experience in Oristano. Oristano is a province in Sardinia and offers a wide array of food markets that provide the ideal open-air shopping experience. The markets are typically noisy but provide plenty of fresh seafood, vegetables and fruit.

Numerous shops lining the streets have a handsome display of handicrafts made by local artisans. These are perfect for securing unusual souvenirs to take home. Bakeries are also plentiful in Oristano. For those with a sweet tooth, you can spend an entire afternoon roaming the bakeries filled with freshly baked pastries as well as homemade candies.

Sapori Di Sadenga

Sapori di Sadenga is situated in the capital Cagliari. It is a small shop that sells some of the best wines and cheeses and other foods at reasonable prices – as well as many local artifacts.

The people working here are knowledgeable about the different foods, cheeses and wines. Whether you are looking to buy a bottle of wine or just to spend the day wine and cheese tasting, Sapori di Sadenga is a perfect shop to do so.

Address: Vico dei Mille, 1, 09125 Cagliari, Sardinia

Phone: 070 6848747

Open: Monday to Saturday

Central Market Alghero

The Central Market in Alghero is popular with both tourists and locals. The bustling market offers everything from Sardinian foods to locally made crafts. For the self-catering traveler in Alghero, this is an ideal shopping place for freshly cut meat, fish, vegetables and fruit.

The market opens on Wednesdays. Simply walk past the Piazza IV Novembre or the main square and follow the crowd heading into Corsa Garibaldi. It is best to arrive at the market before noon to stock up on the freshest Sardinian specialties.

Visitors looking for a selection of local cheese will find them at the Central Market. Several stores also sell jewelry, artworks and books.

Address: Via Sassari, 53 07041 Alghero Province of

Sassari

Phone: 079 9731223

Open: Wednesday

Know Before You Go

 Entry Requirements

By virtue of the Schengen agreement, travellers from other countries in the European Union do not need a visa when visiting Greece. Additionally visitors from certain countries such as Canada, Japan, Israel, Australia, Argentina, Monaco, Andorra, Brazil, Brunei, Chile, Costa Rica, Croatia, Honduras, Guatemala, El Salvador, Nicaragua, Paraguay, Panama, San Marino, Singapore, South Korea, Uruguay, New Zealand and the Vatican State do not need visas if their stay in Greece does not exceed 90 days in a six month period. In the case of travellers from the USA, entry requirements will depend on the type of passport held. While visitors with a normal blue tourist passport will be able to enter the USA without a visa, holders of red official or black diplomatic passports must apply for a Schengen visa prior to departure and will face deportation if attempting to enter Greece without the necessary documentation.

🌍 Health Insurance

Citizens of other EU countries as well as residents from Switzerland, Norway, Iceland, Liechtenstein and the UK are covered for health care in Greece with the European Health Insurance Card (EHIC), which can be applied for free of charge. If you need a Schengen visa for your stay in Greece, you will also be required to obtain proof of health insurance for the duration of your stay (that offers at least €37,500 coverage), as part of your visa application. Visitors from Canada or the USA should check whether their regular health insurance covers travel and arrange for extended health insurance if required.

🌍 Travelling with Pets

Greece participates in the Pet Travel Scheme (PETS) which allows UK residents to travel with their pets without requiring quarantine upon re-entry. Pets travelling between different countries in the EU will need to be accompanied by a valid pet passport, which can be obtained from any licensed veterinarian in the EU. The animal will have to be microchipped and up to date on rabies vaccinations. To visit Greece, your pet will need to be accompanied by a good health certificate issued by a vet no more than ten days prior to your intended departure. The certificate must be in both English and Greek. You should also have a rabies vaccination certificate no less than 30 days and no more than 12 months old. If travelling from a high rabies country, a blood titer test will need to be submitted three months prior to your travel plans. Your animal's microchip should be non-encrypted and compliant with a 15 digit ISO 11784/11785 number (or alternatively you will need to have your own scanner handy.) You will be required to make a declaration of non-commercial travel. If returning to the USA with a pet you adopted in Greece, your pet will need to be vaccinated against rabies at least 30 days prior to entry into the USA.

🌏 Airports

Athens International Airport (ATH) is the busiest airport in Greece. Located about 20km east of the city center, it is the main airport servicing Athens and the region of Attica. **Heraklion International Airport** (HER) is located on the island of Crete, about 5km east of the city of Heraklion. It is the second busiest airport in Greece. **Thessaloniki International Airport** (SKG), also known as Makedonia International Airport, provides access to Khalkidhiki, the region of Macedonia and the northern part of Greece. It is located in Mikra and serves Thessaloniki, the second largest city in Greece. **Rhodes International Airport** (RHO) is located on the western side of the island Rhodes. It is the 4th busiest airport in Greece, providing regular connections to Athens. **Corfu**

International Airport (CFU) is located on the island of Corfu, about 2km south of Corfu City. **Mykonos Island National Airport** (JMK) about 4km from Mykonos Town and **Santorini National Airport** (JTR), provide seasonal connections to the Cyclades at the peak of the summer holidays.

🌐 Airlines

Olympic Airlines, the national flag carrier of Greece for more than 50 years, ceased operation in 2009 due to bankruptcy. From the privatization of its assets, a regional airline, Olympic Air, was formed. Ellinair is a small Greek airline that was established in 2013 and provides regional connections between Athens and Thessaloniki as well as regular flights to Russia, Latvia and the Ukraine. Minoan Air is a small airline based in Heraklion on the island of Crete. It provides connections to Kos and Rhodes, as well as seasonal flights to Santorini and Mytilene. Sky Express is also headquartered in Crete and provides regional connections to 18 Greek destinations. Another Greek airline based in Crete, Bluebird Airways, flies to the Greek destinations of Araxos, Corfu, Kos and Rhodes as well as destinations in Israel, Russia and Turkey.

Athens International Airport serves as a main hub for Aegean Airlines as well as Olympic Air. Olympic Air also uses Rhodes International Airport as a secondary hub. Heraklion International Airport serves as a hub for Bluebird Airways

Minoan Air and Sky Express. It is also a focus city for Aegean Airlines. Thessaloniki International Airport serves as a hub for Aegean Airlines, Astra Airlines, Ellinair and Ryanair.

 Currency

The currency of Greece is the Euro. It is issued in notes in denominations of €500, €200, €100, €50, €20, €10 and €5. Coins are issued in denominations of €2, €1, 50c, 20c, 10c, 5c, 2c and 1c.

Banking & ATMs

You will find ATMs in the larger centers of Greece, although smaller towns may only have a single ATM machine. Greek ATMs are configured for four-digit PIN numbers - make sure your card is compliant before leaving home. However, the financial crisis has introduced an added complication. While daily limits imposed on Greek citizens do not apply to tourists visiting the country, you may encounter ATMs that have run out of cash or banks that are reluctant to exchange pounds for euros. The limits imposed on Greeks will also make it difficult for shop owners to provide change for cash sales. To be on the safe side, consider taking cash in smaller denominations. Do remember to advise your bank of your travel plans before leaving home.

🌍 Credit Cards

The Credit Cards most widely used in Greece are MasterCard and Visa, although American Express is also accepted at more touristy centers. While shops and many hotels accept credit cards, most restaurant options will be limited to cash. Credit card machines in Greece are configured for chip-and-pin type credit cards and you may run into trouble with an older magnetic strip credit card. Greece also has representatives of Western Union, for international money transfers.

🌍 Reclaiming VAT

If you are not from the European Union, you can claim back VAT (Value Added Tax) paid on your purchases in Greece. The VAT rate in Greece is 23 percent, although it varies on certain types of goods and you will qualify for a refund on goods of €120 and over. To reclaim, you must ask the merchant to fill in a refund voucher. You will be asked to show your passport. Make sure that the form is completed and attach your sales slip to the form. The goods must be inspected at the place where you leave the European Union. Here, the necessary documentation will be processed. Your refund will only be valid for items that are still unused at your time of departure. If the merchant is affiliated to Global Refund or Premier Tax Free, you will be able to collect the refund from their offices at the airport in the currency of your choice. A 4 percent service charge will be levied. Alternatively, you could ask for a refund on your credit card or contact the retailer directly, once you have returned home.

🌎 Tipping Policy

At the hotel, tip the porter €1 per bag and the housekeeper €1 per day. At restaurants, you should tip between 5 and 10 percent of the bill, depending on its size. Bear in mind that the service or cover charge on your restaurant bill (usually around €1) is for the table's bread and water. It is customary to tip tour guides in Greece. For a group tour, between €2 and €5 per person is fair. For private tours, €20 per person is the expected rate. On a yacht cruise, tip the captain or skipper between 5 and 15 percent (in a closed envelope) for him to distribute amongst crew members. With taxi drivers, it is customary to round off the amount or to tip between 5 and 10 percent. If you employed a private driver, tip him €20 per day.

🌎 Mobile Phones

Most EU countries, including Greece uses the GSM mobile service. This means that most UK phones and some US and Canadian phones and mobile devices will work in Greece. However, phones using the CDMA network will not be compatible. While you could check with your service provider about coverage before you leave, using your own service in roaming mode will involve additional costs. The alternative is to purchase a Greek SIM card to use during your stay in Greece. Greece has three mobile networks. They are Cosmote, Vodafone and Wind. Of the three networks, Wind is the most economic, but offers the lowest coverage. With each network, you can choose between packages that offer data only or a mixture of voice, text and data. A basic Cosmote SIM with no credit can be purchased for €5, but you will want to look at some of the available package deals as well. Vodafone offers a starter package that includes 2 GB data that can be ordered online for €15, but will cost €20 in store. At Wind you have the choice of a free SIM with top-up cards from €10 or a SIM for €5. They also offer mobile broadband. As per legislation that came into effect in 2009, all Greek SIM cards must be registered before they can be activated. This can only be done in person and you will need to show some form of identification, such as a passport. You can recharge your airtime by buying scratch cards or electronically from ATMs, certain vendors or online with a debit or credit card.

🌐 Dialling Code

The international dialling code for Greece is +30.

🌐 Emergency numbers

General Emergencies: 112

Police: 100

Fire Brigade: 199

Emergency Medical Service: 166

Coast Guard: 108

Emergency Social Assistance: 197

Tourist Police: 171

MasterCard: 00 800 11 887 0303

Visa: 00 800 11 638 0304

🌐 Public Holidays

1 January: New Year's Day

6 January: Day of the Epiphany

February/March: Orthodox Ash Monday

25 March: Independence Day

April (variable): Orthodox Good Friday

April (variable): Orthodox Easter Sunday

April (variable): Orthodox Easter Monday

1 May: Labour Day

May/June: Orthodox Pentecost

May/June: Orthodox Whit Monday

15 August: Assumption Day

28 October: Ochi Day (Oxi Day/Ohi Day)

25 December: Christmas Day

26 December: Second Christmas Day

Time Zone

Greece falls in the Eastern European Time Zone. This can be calculated (from the end of October to the end of March) as follows: Greenwich Mean Time/Coordinated Universal Time (GMT/UTC) +2; Eastern Standard Time (North America) -6; Pacific Standard Time (North America) -9.

Daylight Savings Time

Clocks are set forward one hour on the last Sunday of March and set back one hour on the last Sunday of October for Daylight Savings Time.

School Holidays

The academic year begins in the second week of September and ends in mid June. The summer holiday is from mid June to the first third of September. There are short breaks between Christmas and New Year and also around Easter.

🌐 Trading Hours

In Greece, trading hours vary according to the type of business. You can expect supermarkets to be open from 8am to 8pm on weekdays and until 6pm on Saturdays. Most other shops are open between 9am and 1pm and then again for a late session between 6pm and 9pm. The hours from 1.30pm to 5.30pm are for lunch and siesta, especially in the summer months. Post Offices are open from 8am to 8pm on weekdays and from 8am to 2pm on Saturdays. Shops that cater for tourists may be open until 11pm, especially during the peak tourist season. Pharmacies conform to normal shopping hours, but are usually closed on Saturdays.

🌐 Driving Laws

Greeks drive on the right hand side of the road. A driver's licence from any of the European Union member countries is valid in Greece, but visitors from non-EU countries should apply for an International Driver's License. The minimum driving age in Greece is 18. You will need to have a Green Insurance certificate, also known as a Green Card to cover third party liability and your vehicle needs standard safety gear such as warning triangles, a first aid kit and fire extinguisher. Your vehicle also needs to have headlamp deflectors. The speed limit in Greece is 130km per hour on freeways and 50km an hour on urban roads. The alcohol limit in Greece is under 0.5 g/l. Children under the age of 10 are not allowed to ride in the front seat. It is illegal to use your mobile phone while driving.

🌐 Smoking Laws

Greece is the European country with the highest tobacco consumption rate. As a result, the population has been very tolerant of smoking, even with the introduction of anti-smoking legislation. In fact, business owners have appealed against various forms of anti-smoking laws, arguing that they are bad for business. Smoking in public places has been banned since 2010, but the law provides for bars, taverns, casinos, night clubs and betting shops to create a designated smoking area. It is also illegal to smoke in your car, if in the company of a minor child.

🌐 Drinking Laws

The legal drinking age in Greece is 18. Although Greece has a culture of social drinking, bars and night clubs may state that alcohol will not be served to under 18s or even, in the case of certain cruise tours, under 21s. Alcohol can be bought from supermarkets and even fast food outlets.

 Electricity

Electricity: 230 volts

Frequency: 50 Hz

Greek electricity sockets use the Type F plugs, which feature two round pins or prongs. They are also compatible with Type C and Type E plugs. If travelling from the USA, you will need a power converter or transformer to convert the voltage from 230 to 110, to avoid damage to your appliances. The latest models of many laptops, camcorders, mobile phones and digital cameras are dual-voltage with a built in converter.

Tourist Information (TI)

There are three National Tourist Offices in the city of Athens where you can pick up maps of the city, as well as time tables for the Greek bus, train and ferry services. They are located at Athens Eleftherios Venizelos Airport, in the Athens Center at 26A Amalias Avenue and 7 Tsoha Street.

Food & Drink

Greek cuisine relies heavily on the use of olive oil (and olives), cheese and aubergines (or eggplant). Beef is rare, but there are plenty of lamb and pork dishes to make up for it. One of the most popular Greek dishes is moussaka, a casserole consisting of layers of eggplant and spiced mince. Try the baked pasta dish, pastitsio or if you like meat stews, do make sure that you try stifado as well. With an abundance of seafood available, don't forget to enjoy the abundance of grilled fish and octopus. A course of small meze dishes is often served as appetizer or to accompany a round of drinks. The standard meze favorites include tzatziki (a dip of yoghurt and cucumber), hummus (made of chickpea), dolmades, keftedes, olives, feta cheese and taramasalata (a fish roe dip), usually served with pita or flatbread. Another delicious appetizer is saganaki, or fried cheese, often made with halloumi, kefalotyri, graviera, kefalograviera or feta. Graviera, which is a native product of Crete, is the second most popular cheese in Greece after feta. Fast and meaty snacks to enjoy on the go are souvlaki (meat skewers), kebabs or gyros - pitas filed with meat, French fries and smothered in tzatziki. Phyllo pastry is used for a variety of dishes, including the standard dessert of baklava and tiropitakia (or cheese pies). If you happen to find yourself on Mykonos, do make sure you sample kopanisti, a cheesy appetizer, a few slices of louza, the local salami and some amigthalota, to indulge your sweet tooth. Crete is a must for cheese lovers, where practically every village has its own distinctive varieties. Here you can also enjoy Askordoulakous or "mountain bulbs", lamb with stamnagathi or sfakia pies. For a taste of manouri - a cheese similar to feta with a creamier character - you need to be in Thessaly or Macedonia.

The most popular beers local beer in Greece is Mythos, although Amstel and Heineken are also available at most venues. Retsina is the type of wine most often associated with Greece, although its distinctive taste of resin is not all that popular with foreigners. Another popular drink is ouzo, a strong liquor with a minty taste that combines well with seafood. If visiting Epirus, Macedonia or Crete, to sample the local raki and tsipouro, which is served in small shot glasses. If you want to quench your thirst with something refreshing and non-alcoholic, try soumada, a Cretan beverage of almond and rose water.

 Websites

http://www.visitgreece.gr/

http://www.greeka.com/best-greece-destinations.htm

http://www.greek-tourism.gr/

http://wikitravel.org/en/Greece

http://www.visit-ancient-greece.com/

http://www.greektravel.com/mainland.htm

Printed in Great Britain
by Amazon

38246283R00046